But what you got was poo

And crying, 2am feeds, sick on your shoulder, a partner who doesn't understand, constant exhaustion, career affected, and a guilty feeling that you're supposed to be on top of the world about this.

When you're not.

The thing is, what you're feeling isn't unnatural or even unusual. You haven't 'failed', no-one is going to take your child away and it doesn't mean you're a bad mother or you've got a terrible baby. Instead, it means the fairy tales are exaggerated and you're a lot closer to reality than those film stars who talk about fulfillment and get back to size 8 within a week.

You do need to sort out your feelings, though.
And if you think it would also help to get some sleep, find some energy, stop feeling overwhelmed, rediscover the old you and lay the foundations for a lovely relationship with your baby, you've come to the right book.

So, let's start by working out what makes you feel bad.

, choose a
e when you
el worse,
en ask...

What's going on?

Lots of things change when you have a baby. Many are positive - feeling happy and relaxed. But at times you may feel bad, stressed, down and out of balance in key areas of your life.

These include:

Altered thinking: You want to be positive and in control, but at times it doesn't seem this way and you feel over-whelmed. Are any of the following familiar?

"There's too much to do."

"I'm so tired I can't cope."

"I'll never get the hang of this."

"I'm such a useless mother."

"I don't feel attractive any more."

Altered feelings: If you beat yourself up mentally and think like this, it alters how you feel. You may feel bad - stressed, low, irritable, ashamed, guilty or weepy.

These strong emotions can have an impact on how you cope physically.

Altered physical symptoms: You may not be sleeping well. Pain from a C-section, an episiotomy or a tear make you feel even worse. Your breasts may ache, or your nipples feel painful. You feel exhausted, aren't sleeping well, and stress makes you feel even worse.

Altered behaviours: And all of these changes add up to affect your activity levels, so you find it harder to do things. You may try and cope by cutting down what you do, trying to make it through. But the less you do, the worse you feel, and the worse you feel, the less you do.

And you know what happens then?

YOU FALL INTO A VICIOUS CIRCLE

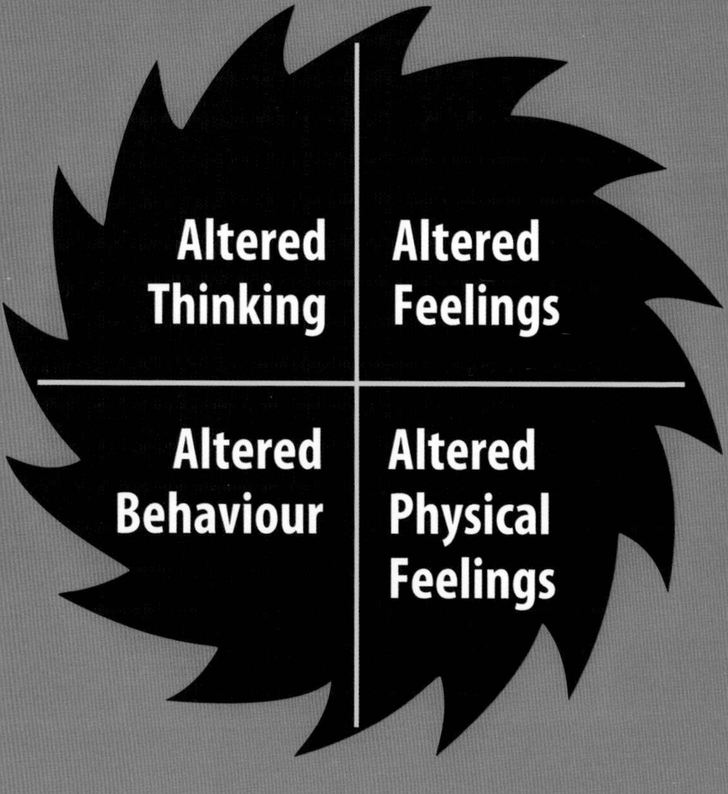

Altered Thinking

Altered Feelings

Altered Behaviour

Altered Physical Feelings

And the circle spins, making you feel worse and worse.

We've looked at four key areas that can change when you feel bad – thinking, emotional and physical feelings and behaviour There's a fifth area to consider too- the people and events around you. That's the area outside the circle on the diagram.

What events make you feel bad?

Well it might be your baby waking crying for the fourth time tonight.
Or your friend saying "my baby could do this or that by this time."
Or "helpful" advise from people, or too much to do, or not enough money.

There may also be other things going on in life like bills to pay, jobs to do, other children, housework, not to mention maintaining relationships and friendships.
And all the demands can build up.

These things outside you can make you feel bad inside too by making the circle spin.
You may start to change what you do in ways that backfire. Are you pushing people away? Being rude to people who care for you? Or isolating yourself, not asking for the help you need? Perhaps you lean on drink or drugs to cope when you know that's bad for you and your baby?

So...

WHAT ABOUT YOU?

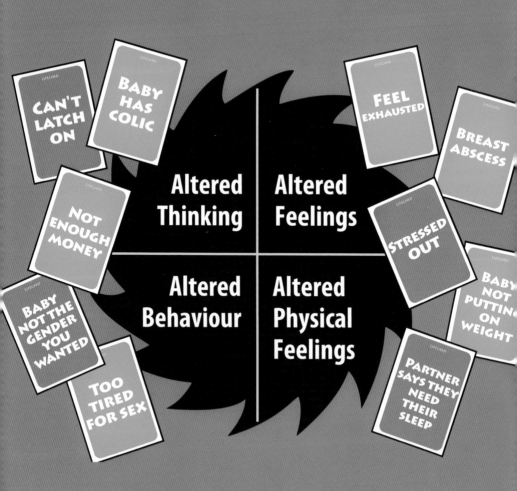

CAN'T LATCH ON

BABY HAS COLIC

NOT ENOUGH MONEY

BABY NOT THE GENDER YOU WANTED

TOO TIRED FOR SEX

Altered Thinking

Altered Behaviour

Altered Feelings

Altered Physical Feelings

FEEL EXHAUSTED

BREAST ABSCESS

STRESSED OUT

BABY NOT PUTTING ON WEIGHT

PARTNER SAYS THEY NEED THEIR SLEEP

Complete your own five areas assessment

Do you fall into vicious circles from time to time? Here's how to play detective and work out how the vicious circle affects you.

Choose two recent times when you felt bad. To start with don't pick times that are really upsetting or distressing. Instead choose situations when you feel a bit down, fed up, stressed, scared, frustrated, guilty, ashamed, exhausted, or in pain.

Use the next two pages to work out how you reacted.

Pen at the ready?

Now it's time to spot that vicious circle.

People and Events

Altered
Thinking

People and
Events

Altered
Behaviour

People and Events

Altered
Feelings

Altered Physical
Feelings

People and
Events

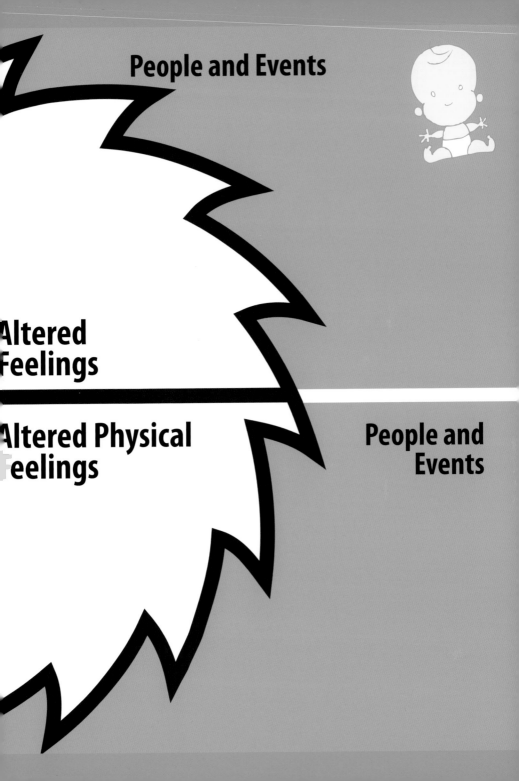

HOW TO CHANGE THINGS AROUND

14 changes to help you feel better

To enjoy your baby more, you need to make 14 changes to your life. There are some things that are immediately good for building your relationship with your baby, some that are especially good for you, and finally one's that help you change how you respond to others.

You can't make them all at once of course, but if you change one thing at a time, then you and your baby will start to feel happier.

So this is what to do:
Every time you turn a couple of pages in this book, we'll suggest one change to your life, your thoughts, your routine, or your relationships. There are 14 changes altogether.

Start by making a cup of tea and reading the book all the way through, thinking about the 14 changes, scribbling notes in the margins.

There is a section at the end of the book to help you make some effective plans to change how things are.

Now, let's find out about the first change you can make.

Turn over for some changes that are good for your baby.

CHANGE 1: GOO GOO DAY

Today you're going to make a lot of silly noises

Babies don't know what you're saying but they love to hear you saying it. They really like it when you look in their eyes and they think you're fantastic when you pull silly faces or play peek-a-boo.

Of course, no-one can cope with goo-goo noises all day long, not you and not your baby, so the best bet is to do it in 15 minute bursts, five or six times a day.

You can do it while changing or bathing, or after a sleep. You can also do it with toys, of course. But don't rush out and empty the toyshop. Banging a spoon on a plastic cup is the baby equivalent of an X-Box One!

Sometimes, you may notice your baby looking away from you in the middle of a play session. This isn't boredom, it's thinking. Babies' brains have to take in so much brand new stuff that occasionally, they need a pause to sort it all out.

Here's the baby top 5 of games to play with mum:

1. Peek-a-boo.

2. Singing nursery rhymes while having hands clapped gently.

3. Banging things to make a noise.

4. Copycat – watching mum pull silly faces as she copies my expressions.

5. Splashing water in the bath.

Make every day a goo-goo day and you and your baby will really enjoy each other.

CHANGE 2: STORY DAY

Your baby was born loving books

Although babies don't understand words, they understand sounds very well. And when you read a book to your baby, you're sending some of the loveliest sound messages there are.

Face your baby while reading, so that he or she can see your eyes and your expression. Being able to see the book is also a good idea and don't be surprised if your baby reaches out for it.

Try and have one reading session a day, and don't worry about having to buy a lot of books, there are plenty at the library.

Of course, you might think "If baby doesn't understand words, what's wrong with reading the same book over and over?" There's nothing to stop you doing that, but instead why not give yourself some variety!

Although today may be the first time you try reading to baby, do think about making it part of the daily routine. As baby grows up, you could form your own little book group and even invite other mums and babies as well!

CHANGE 3: RELAX

TAKE A HOLIDAY

When you feel stress rising, take a mental step back. Slow things down. Drop your shoulders down (they tend to rise up towards your ears if you get tense). And breathe. Close your mouth and breathe with the lower part of your chest - taking normal size breaths through your nose. (Ignore all those comments about taking a deep breath).

You can get free MP3 relaxation downloads as part of the Living Life to the Full course at www.llttf.com, or use any other relaxation technique that works for you.

CHANGE 4: DO DAY

Today, you're going to make a new routine

Having to get out of bed to get your baby up, dressed and fed can be a real pain, especially on cold mornings when you haven't slept much. But having a routine can really help.

First get yourself up - get showered and dressed. Make a clear start to the day so you're not wandering round the house in a nightie or dressing gown all day.

After the baby and you are up, then make yourself a routine with other things. Making a pot of coffee. Listening to the radio. Cleaning the house. Popping to the corner shop to say hello and buy some fruit. Phoning a friend. Walking in the park with the pram with friends.

It needs to be a daily routine and, of course, it needs to fit in with your baby's feed and change times.

It must also contain more than chores. That walk, that sit down with the radio or a book, that phone call with mum or a friend – they're all as important as the washing up (actually, they're more important).

So sit and think, get a pen and use the Activity Planner over the page to plan your days from now on.

My activity planner

Plan a balance of activities over the days and week. Choose things you Value and give a sense of Pleasure, Achievement or Closeness.
Build things up over a few weeks so you end up with one activity planned in each part of the day. Leave some gaps for the unexpected things that crop up. Have some time just for you.
Get into a routine- a time to get up, eat, go to bed, and do the household chores, or perhaps to go for a walk, meet friends or attend a regular class.

Plan in the key essentials that otherwise will build up and cause you problems- paying bills, cutting the lawn, doing the washing up, ironing, having a hair cut etc.

MY ACTIVITY

	Monday	Tuesday	Wednesday
Morning			
Afternoon			
Evening			

PLANNER

Thursday	Friday	Saturday	Sunday

NOW HERE ARE SOME THINGS TO ADD INTO YOUR ACTIVITY PLANNER

Work out what makes you feel good

Write down all the things you've enjoyed, have given you a sense of pleasure or achievement, or helped you feel close to someone.

Things I enjoy:

_____

_____

Things I've done/achieved:

_____

_____

Things that make me feel close to others:

_____

_____

What about essential activities that you need to do?

_____

_____

How much do your activities fit with your values/ideals of how you want to live your life?

_____

_____

Pick activities that make you feel good, and start to plan them into the *Activity Planner* across the days and week.

Next, you're going to build on these activities.

Next, you're going to re-connect with people. Even if you don't feel like it

We often avoid people when we're feeling down. We're bound up with our own troubles and can't be bothered getting out of the house to talk to anyone else. Even phoning a friend can seem too hard to do.

But loneliness just makes you feel worse and worse, so try this today:
Think about some good times you used to have with friends, before baby came along. Remember the laughs you had and the way you used to talk and talk.

Hold those thoughts, phone a friend and ask if you can come round with your baby. If they are free, get ready and go there now or arrange to meet another time.

When you get back, ring your baby clinic or doctor's surgery and ask about the next mums and tots meeting. Decide to go to it. No arguments. Choose to go.

Once you've done these things, do them again, at least once a week. And then think about widening your circle of friends that you visit regularly. It'll do you good and all this socialising is great for baby, too.

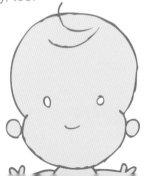

Get going physically. Go for a walk today, for an hour

Then do it again, at least once a week

People who recover from really bad times often say they appreciate things they used to take for granted. So get your coat on and your baby all wrapped up and take a 60-minute walk. Go see the world for the amazing place that it is.

Even better, do it with a friend or your partner. Try and walk somewhere pretty or interesting. Or change your route regularly so there's variety and always something to talk about.

While you're walking, really notice what's around you. The wind, the warmth, the cold, the trees, the flowers, the shops and the sky. Pretend you're seeing them for the first time, like your baby, and point them out in a loud, positive voice. He or she won't have the faintest idea what you're on about, but you'll both feel closer and happier. Your voice is the best noise on earth, remember? Some prams allow you to have your baby face you as you walk. Your baby will love that as you're the most exciting thing in the world to them just now.

You'll both feel better almost straight away, we promise.

PAMPER DAY

Today, you're going to be good to yourself

Get your nails done. Spend a bit extra on your hair. Have a facial, a foot spa, a head massage, a sauna. You'll feel so much better and your baby will notice that you're happier and more relaxed.

Of course, you'll have to get a friend or partner signed up for a bit of babysitting, but they'll soon start to volunteer their services when they notice how much better you are when you come back.

Can't afford to pay for fancy treatments? Then fix up with a girlfriend to be each other's nail specialist or Reiki expert.

Get the stuff you need from a basics range at the supermarket, look up the techniques online or at the library and you'll probably have even more laughs doing it this way than at the local salon, and you may not even need the babysitting service.

GO OUT DAY

Today, leave your baby with someone you trust and have some *You Time.*

Just getting away from your baby for an hour or so is a good way to get life back into perspective. And when you make it a regular outing, it becomes something you can really look forward to.
Of course, you'll need to keep it short at first, especially if you're breast feeding. But as you and your baby (and your babysitter) get into the routine, you could stretch to half a day or so eventually.
There's just one rule you must stick to – go somewhere that YOU want to go. No duty visits to relatives. No catching up on errands or food shopping. Other times are for those things you need to do.

Window shop for clothes, see an old friend, watch sport, walk in the park, go to the pictures or the library, treat yourself to tea and a bun with a friend.
If you feel a bit guilty at first, or miss your baby, don't worry. This is natural and you'll soon get over it as you start to really enjoy your trips. You'll also be brighter and nicer for your baby when you get back.
Go out days are really important because they help you to find yourself and see things more clearly. Make sure you diary it for at least one a fortnight from now on.

CHANGE 8: LOOKING AFTER YOU

SOME TIPS ON STAYING HAPPY

Doing things that give you a sense of pleasure, achievement or closeness to people can help improve how you feel. There are also plenty of other things you can do that will help to keep your spirits up for good.

Choose activities that help you get fitter as well as happier. Here are some ideas:

Happy Steps

Exercise is good for you. So good that when you do it, your body says 'thanks' by sending happy chemicals to your brain. But who's got the time or money to go to the gym?

Instead, use the stairs rather than the lift or escalator when you're out. Climbing stairs with a pram or buggy is one of the best ways there is to get fitter and get that happy stuff into your head.

Decide to do it next time you're out. Then decide to keep on doing it and always take the stairs. Your brain will get happier and happier.

Make a Note of This

Music cheers you up. Obvious? So why are you sitting there in silence if you find silence is just a space for you to think about your worries in?

Put some of your favourite music on. Do it now. Play music while you're bathing baby or doing the dishes. Play music while you're walking briskly to the shops. Play music while you're sitting around.

But don't play sad music, or songs that remind you of unhappy times. Keep it upbeat and you'll get an instant lift.

Take One Away

Eating too much fast food or takeaway food is a great way to get really down.

Did you see that experiment where a man ate nothing but fast food? He felt depressed and really unhealthy inside a couple of weeks.

So here's what you do: cut out one take-away a week. Just one. Replace it with something you make yourself (easy things like beans on toast are fine).

Within just a week or so, you'll start to feel lighter, fitter and happier. And a bit better off.

CHANGE 9: THE HAPPY LIST

Time to remember

When you're down it's easy to forget the good times. The times you've succeeded in something, happy times with friends and baby, things that make you smile.

So remember them. Each evening, sit down and write down three things that you:

- **have enjoyed**

- **felt was a job well done**

- **or helped you feel close to someone else**

After a few days, you'll have a list of great things that you can look back on, and this will help you feel a lot better.

MY HAPPY LIST

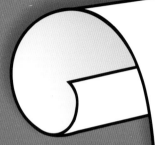

Write down all
the things you've
enjoyed, gave
you a sense of
achievement, or
helped you feel
close to someone.
How much did it
fit with your
values/ideals
of how you
want to live
your life?

What are
you
thankful
for today?

CHANGE 10: THOUGHTS DAY

Today, let's get your thinking sorted out

When you're feeling low, the way you think can make you worse. You may beat yourself up for not being a good mother or for leaving the housework. Maybe you assume others think badly of you, or perhaps you take responsibility for everything.

From now on, we're going to call all these things 'Bad Thoughts'. Because they're not helpful, they're usually not true and they just get you down.

Sit quietly for a few minutes with this little chart and tick the kind of bad thoughts that you've had in the last few days.

Are you your own worst critic?
Do you always seem to be beating yourself up about something?

Do you focus on the bad stuff?
As if you were looking at the world through darkened glasses?

Do you have a gloomy view of the future?
Expecting everything to turn out badly.

Are you jumping to the worst conclusions?
It's called 'catastrophising'.

Do you assume that others see you badly?
When you haven't checked whether it's true, it's called 'mind-reading'.

Do you take responsibility for everything?
Including things that aren't your fault.

Are you always saying things like 'Should' 'Ought to' 'Got to'?
Setting impossible standards for yourself?

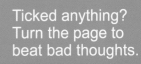

Ticked anything?
Turn the page to
beat bad thoughts.

THE AMAZING BAD THOUGHT BUSTING PROGRAMME

1. Label the thought

When you notice one of your bad thoughts, mentally step back and stick a label on it. "Oh, that's just one of those bad thoughts".

When you label a bad thought this way, it loses its power and you realise that it's just part of being upset. It's not the truth, it's just one of those bad thoughts.

You could even talk to it. Say: "You're rumbled! I'm not playing that game again!"

2. Leave the thought alone

Mentally turn your back on the bad thought.

Don't challenge it or try to argue with it, just let it be. A bad thought loves attention, so don't give it any.

Instead, think about what you're doing right now or are planning for the future, or things you've achieved lately.

3. Stand up to the thought

Bad thoughts are like bullies. They sound strong but really they're weak underneath. And they tell lies.

They say you won't like doing something. They say you'll fail if you try. They tell you you're useless or you're scared or nobody likes you.

But this is just the bad thought, not the truth. Don't be bullied!

4. Give yourself a break

Bad thoughts are how we beat ourselves up when we're upset. So if you're having trouble with a bad thought, think what the person who loves you most in the world would say to you, right now.

They'd disagree with the bad thoughts, wouldn't they? They'd remind you that you're great and most certainly not a failure or a bad mother.

Trust this person that loves you and watch the bad thoughts fade away.

5. Look at it differently

Some bad thoughts keep coming back and you wonder if you'll ever get the better of them.

Here are four things you can do that will help.
Give yourself some good advice
Imagine what it would be like if it was a friend, not you, who was having this bad thought. What advice would you give? Now give the same advice to yourself. Do you apply one set of standards to yourself and a different one to others? Why?

Put your thought or worry into perspective
Does it really matter so much? Will it matter in six months? Will you even remember what the problem was? If it won't matter in six months, it's probably not that important now!

How would others deal with the problem?
Think about someone who seems to handle problems well and work out what they would do, or how they would think in this situation.

Think about the facts, not your feelings
Sometimes you think bad things because you're feeling low. Then the bad thoughts make you feel even worse. Try to look past the bad thoughts and get to the truth.

You're not going to sleep like a baby

But these simple rules will help you have a better night

It takes most babies at least 6 weeks to start to get into a feeding/ sleeping routine. So the best thing to do in that time is help the process along by starting each day at the same time and trying to feed and change them at regular intervals.

Take your own naps when you can and, of course, get friends and partners roped in on the housework etc.

As things start to settle down, you should be able to take your own sleep needs more seriously, so here are some ideas that you can start working on today and build into a regular routine.

These things work

Be good to yourself and gently wind down for half an hour before bed. Have a bath with bubbles or salts, sip a nice warm milky drink and listen to some soothing music. If you find that reading relaxes you, read *The Secrets of the Baby Whisperer* by Tracy Hogg – it has some great ideas in it.

Make sure your bedroom is warm, cosy and dark. If the bed is chilly, add a blanket or another duvet, and go back to the hot water bottle you used to love as a kid.

Is the bed really comfy? If not, change your pillows and try turning the mattress. Curtains a bit thin? Try thicker ones or blackout linings. Things a bit noisy outside? Get some earplugs from the chemist (test them out first, making sure you can still hear baby).

These don't

Exercise is a bad idea just before bed. Getting physically tired might seem OK, but actually, it's not as good as slowly winding down. Don't do anything strenuous near bedtime.

Don't smoke, either. Smoking wakes you up. Have your last cigarette half an hour before your bath.

TV is also a no-no. Watch it to calm down before your bath but get rid of the TV in your bedroom. Lose the radio too, or at least, don't listen to it before sleeping. And take those books downstairs - reading in bed is also against the rules, as is eating.

Alcohol seems as if it makes you sleepy, but it's just a shallow sleep that doesn't last for long and you'll probably have to get up for the loo. Don't have a drink in the hour before bed.

Today you're going to become more assertive

First, let's get something straight. Being assertive isn't the same as being demanding, rude or aggressive. It's simply having the confidence and self-respect to tell others what you need and how you feel, and to say no – quietly but firmly – when you can't go along with something.

It takes practice to be assertive, especially if you've spent years avoiding confrontation and putting other people's needs before your own. But it can be done and there are a couple of simple techniques you can try straight away.

The broken record

This works in almost every situation. First, before you talk to anyone else, practice what you want to say by repeating over and over again what you want or need. So, "sorry, I can't do that this week", "sorry but I just can't do that this week" "I'm so sorry, but I can't help with that this week.

When you've learned your 'lines', simply keep on returning to them throughout the conversation, stating your wishes clearly and calmly until you get what you want.

Saying 'no'

You may think saying 'no' will upset people or make them not like you, but the opposite is often true if you say it the right way – calmly and firmly, and repeating it, like the broken record method above.

Go on – try it now. "No. I won't be able to do that today." "No, I have other things to see to at the moment."

Start to use this important little word today and you'll be surprised what a difference it can make.

Now turn the page, we're going to read you your rights…

THE 12 RULES OF ASSERTIVENESS

I have the right to:

1. Respect myself – who I am and what I do.

2. Recognise my own needs as an individual – separate from what's expected of me as a mother, daughter, wife, partner.

3. Make clear 'I' statements about how I feel and what I think – for example 'I feel uncomfortable with your decision.'

4. Allow myself to make mistakes – it's normal.

5. Change my mind – if I choose to.

6. Ask for 'thinking about it' time – when people ask you to do something, you have the right to say 'I'd like to think it over. I'll let you know by the end of the week.'

7. Allow myself to enjoy my successes – being pleased with what I've done and sharing it with others.

8. Ask for what I want – rather than hoping someone will notice what I want.

9. Recognise that I am not responsible for the behaviour of other adults – or for pleasing other adults all the time.

10. Respect other people – and their right to be assertive and expect the same in return.

11. Say 'I don't understand.'

12. Deal with others – without depending on them for approval.

CHANGE 13: CHILL DAY

Today, you're going to simmer down

Everyone gets irritable from time to time, but if you find yourself flying off the handle too often, here's a system that really works.

It's all about understanding your hot buttons and changing what you do in tense situations. We call it the *1,2,3, Breathe!* method.

1. Know your buttons

Think about what makes you cross. When your partner isn't helping. When you're being pulled apart by too many demands. When your baby just can't be comforted. Know your buttons and you can keep them from being pressed.

Take a few minutes and write them here.

2. Know your early warning system

You feel different just before you snap. With some people it's heavy breathing. Others clench their fists or feel tears welling up. Or maybe your early warnings are in your mind. You start to feel critical of someone else. You don't think much of their voice, their opinions. Maybe you feel ignored or think people are looking down on you.

What do you feel just before exploding? Make a note here.

3. Know your escape hatches

An escape hatch gets you out of a bad situation. You might just walk away, or pause and count to 10. Other people hum a little tune (music from your favourite film maybe?). When you know a few escape hatches, you can stay in control whatever happens.

Here are some ideas:

Smile.
When your face or fists are tensing up, make yourself give out a proper big smile that lights up your face. Others will notice, and things will calm down.

Relax your shoulders.
Notice where your shoulders are and make a point of relaxing and letting them drop while you slow down your breathing.

Sit down.
It's a lot harder to explode when you're sitting down, so when you get an early warning, stay in your seat, or go find one.

Hum.
We're serious. You can't easily shout and scream when you're humming – especially a slow, calming tune.

NOW Breathe!

Drop your shoulders, close your mouth and breathe normal sized breaths at a normal pace.
It's worked! You've escaped and stayed in control, so you can give yourself respect. You used the *1,2,3, Breathe!* method to avoid an outburst and life is nicer for you and everyone else around you!

45

CHANGE 14: TIME TO SORT THINGS OUT

When things mount up, they get you down

Piles of ironing or unpaid bills just add to your unhappy feelings.

Although it's hard to face things when they mount up, sorting them out will really lift your mood.

So, when problems occur with the people and events around you, you need to think how to tackle them.

But where do you start?

Use the Easy 4 step plan to make your changes

Changing things in your life is never easy, especially big or complicated things, so you need a system that can handle almost anything.

The Easy 4 Step Plan helps you break things down so that you can really get them done and, as you may have guessed, has four simple steps.

Here are the first two:

1. Break the problem into pieces

It's hard to stop doing something all at once, especially if you've been doing it for ages, so break it into easy chunks.

Let's say you want to cut down smoking. You could break the week into bits and decide just to stop on Mondays, for example.

If your problem is hiding away from the world, don't try and become a party animal yet - just work on a little bit of the problem - like getting out of the house.

Or if you're eating too much, start by just cutting out cakes or crisps.

Most problems can be chopped up like this, and you're much more likely to succeed when you do things bit by bit.

2. Brainstorm ways to do the first piece

Grab a piece of paper and write down all the things you could do to work on the first bit of the problem.

If you're working on getting out of the house, you might buy a book on trees and try and spot four new types every day as you walk with your baby through the park (explaining about the different leaves in a loud, friendly voice!)

Trying to cut down online shopping? Use the parental controls in your browser to lock yourself out of whatever sites you spend money on.

The trick with brainstorming is to let your mind go, and write everything down - the whacky things as well as the sensible ones.

Do this and there's bound to be a good idea in there somewhere.

3. Choose an idea and make a plan to do it

Look at your brainstorm ideas and pick one. Choose one that looks do-able and doesn't scare you too much.

Now take another piece of paper and write down, step by step, how to actually DO it.

Make the steps as small as you like: Get up. Get dressed. Get baby ready. Walk to front door. Open door….and so on.

Make sure that the steps are small, straightforward and seem like things you could really do.

4. Check the plan and put it into action

Five ticks?
Then *Go For It!*

PLAN, DO AND REVIEW

Make changes one step at a time

OK. You've read about all the 14 changes that you can make, scribbled notes in the margins and maybe thought about what you might like to do first. Now it's time to actually start feeling better.

You need to plan *what* you are going to do, and *when* you're going to do each change, and in what order.

The *Planner sheet* on pages 52/53 will help you make an effective plan.

Then use the *Review sheet* on pages 54/55 to learn from what happens.

Use them to make better and better plans. Try to get into a cycle of *Plan*, *Do* and *Review* to help you move forwards.

Good Luck!

DON'T JUST SIT THERE, MAKE A PLAN!

1. WHAT AM I GOING TO DO?

2. WHEN AM I GOING TO DO IT?

3. WHAT PROBLEMS OR DIFFICULTIES COULD ARISE, AND HOW CAN I OVERCOME THEM?

Is my planned task

Q. USEFUL FOR UNDERSTANDING OR CHANGING HOW I AM?

YES ☐ NO ☐

Q. SPECIFIC, SO THAT I WILL KNOW WHEN I HAVE DONE IT?

YES ☐ NO ☐

Q. REALISTIC, PRACTICAL AND ACHIEVABLE?

YES ☐ NO ☐

MY NOTES

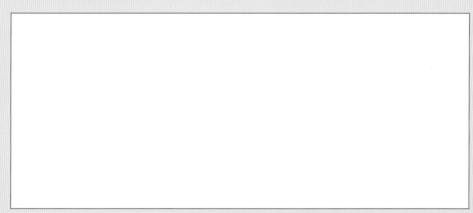

OK, HOW DID IT GO?

WHAT DID YOU PLAN TO DO?
WRITE IT HERE

DID YOU TRY TO DO IT?

YES   NO

☐   ☐

IF YES:
1. WHAT WENT WELL?

2. WHAT DIDN'T GO SO WELL?

3. WHAT HAVE YOU LEARNED FROM WHAT HAPPENED?

4. HOW ARE YOU GOING TO APPLY WHAT YOU HAVE LEARNED?

IF NO: WHAT STOPPED YOU?

INTERNAL THINGS
(FORGOT, NOT ENOUGH TIME, PUT IT OFF, DIDN'T THINK I COULD DO IT, COULDN'T SEE THE POINT ETC.).

EXTERNAL THINGS
(OTHER PEOPLE, WORK OR HOME ISSUES ETC.).

HOW COULD YOU HAVE PLANNED TO TACKLE THESE THINGS?

BUT BEFORE YOU FINISH, WE WANT YOUR FRIENDS TO CALL YOU NAMES

'Talkative' will do for starters

There are no circumstances, ever, when it's better to keep quiet when you're feeling down.

Although you might want to hide away and 'just get through it', this won't work. You'll feel better sooner if you talk to someone.

A friend is good. Or a parent, partner, colleague, counsellor. Do it now - open up with someone you trust – someone you may have been shutting out lately.

What to talk about? Talk about yourself. Explain how you're unhappy, confused, scared, exhausted, irritated.

Ask for help with household chores, feeding or changing baby, taking over for an hour or so, taking the other kids off your hands for a while, going for a walk with you, or just coming round and listening.

If you're feeling desperate, ring your doctor or the emergency services, or go to the local Accident and Emergency department.

The aim of talking is to get support, but you'll also get another benefit – talking about problems tends to sort them out in your head. You'll understand things better and get ready for change.

Talking is something you need to make daily. Do a lot of it today, but also decide to do some of it every day from now on.

HOW FAMILY AND FRIENDS CAN HELP

SHOW THIS BIT TO THE PEOPLE YOU'RE CLOSE TO

Hi, thanks for reading this!

Your part in my plan includes understanding, listening and some practical stuff.

First, have a look through the rest of the book and get to know the 14 changes. You'll spot that some of them can't be done alone. There's help needed with bathing baby, household chores, baby sitting and going for walks – so get ready to be called on for some of that!

Also, you'll need to polish up your listening skills so that you can really help when talking about mum's feelings.

You might want to do a bit of research, too. Reading about issues like post-natal depression online or getting some books out of the library will help you understand things and be even more useful.

Supporting someone sounds straightforward, but it isn't always. You may get irritated or frustrated. You may say or do things that you think are helpful, but don't seem to work. It's even possible to make things worse without realising it.

Don't get discouraged though, just turn the page for a quick checklist on the Do's and Don'ts of helping.

THIS IS HELPFUL

'Being there' for mum in the long term.

Being willing to talk and offer support when needed.

Being happy to help with household and baby chores.

Encouraging mum to ask questions of the health visitor and other experts.

Encouraging mum to make this 14-day plan and stick to it.

Having a sense of humour and using it to help mum cope.

Staying positive but realistic – things will get better, but there are no quick fixes.

Helping mum to pace her recovery – she'll get better bit by bit, so don't let her take on too much too soon.

Staying well yourself by taking time out and getting advice from your doctor or a counsellor if necessary.

Encouraging mum to seek extra help when it's needed – or to call on others if you have big concerns that she and her baby aren't getting the help they need.

THIS ISN'T

(Even though it may be well meant)

Wrapping mum in cotton wool. You mustn't take over everything.

Bullying or nagging. Advice is great. Constantly telling mum what to do isn't.

Shouting. If you feel frustrated with the way things are going, imagine how mum feels. Stay calm. Read pages 44 to 45 of this book.

Being there' too much. Yes, it's possible. If mum is always on the phone to you or feels that she can't cope without constantly getting reassurance from someone, t's a problem.

Being unrealistic. Too many breezy statements like you'll be fine – don't worry!' or 'everything will work out!' eventually can make it seem as if you're not taking things seriously if there are problems like postnatal depression present.

Avoiding the issue. People are different. The chance to talk about things can help. If mum wants this, gently encourage her to talk about her feelings and help her by listening without immediately offering solutions.

HOW TO GET EVEN MORE HELP

If you're really not coping and feel very depressed it's time to say 'enough is enough' and get help. If you're worried that you might harm your baby or yourself, please take action now.

Arrange to see your GP, tell your health visitor or contact one of these helpful groups. No-one will judge or criticise you and everyone will do their best to help.

Your own GP
or the Accident and Emergency department at your local hospital

The Samaritans (24 hours)
Telephone 0845 7 90 90 90 or Email: jo@samaritans.org

NHS 24 for Scotland (24 hours)
Telephone 111

NHS Direct for England and Wales (24 hours)
Telephone 111

Breathing Space (Scotland)
6pm - 2am (Monday to Thursday)
6pm - 6am at weekends (Friday, Saturday, Sunday)
Telephone 0800 83 85 87

Help in Northern Ireland

The Samaritans
5 Wellesley Avenue
BELFAST BT9 6DG
County Antrim
Telephone: 028 90664422

Lifeline
Telephone: 0808 808 8000 for people of all ages in crisis or despair.